AF337278

CLIMATE DENIAL

Henri Landes - Thomas Porcher

CLIMATE DENIAL

Max Milo
ESSAIS-DOCUMENTS

Max Milo Editions
Collection Essais-Documents, Paris, 2023
www.maxmilo.com
ISBN : 978-2-315-01147-6

Introduction

A few weeks before the 21st Climate Change Conference (COP 21[1]) in Paris, this book makes the uncompromising observation that we are all climate skeptics.

Of course, we are different from Claude Allègre and the traditional climate skeptics because we recognize the causes and consequences of global warming. We are well aware that the source of the problem comes from human activity and we also clearly identify the consequences, such as recurrent extreme weather events, the melting of the ice cap or the tens of millions of climate refugees every year around the world. Yet, knowingly, we refuse to change our production and consumption patterns. No matter how many conferences and alarming reports there are, no matter if they come from the IPCC, the UN or the World Bank, we refuse to consider

---

1. See keywords at the end of the book.

this reality. This climate denial is a new form of climate skepticism, one that consists in recognizing global warming as a fact, without acting accordingly.

This observation is visible at different levels. It can be seen in the inability of our governments to reach agreement when all the indicators are red. It is visible in the energy we consume, which is still more than 80% polluting. It is in our measurement indicators which only take into account market production without taking into account pollution and the destruction of natural resources. It is also in the hundreds of free trade agreements, active or in the process of being signed, which promote the exchange of goods throughout the world without the slightest clause on the climate.

How much longer can we remain locked in this hypo-critical posture that consists of constantly subtracting the climate constraint from our decisions so as not to have to question our economic model? Can we, for example, on the one hand debate the exploitation of shale gas and on the other promote the fight against global warming? Can we still rejoice in having oil reserves for more than a hundred years when extracting more than a third of them would be dramatic for the climate? Can we promote trade in the world through free trade treaties when CO2 emissions must fall in the next five years to meet the 2°C target[2] ? Or can we still

---

2. Limiting global warming to 2°C compared to the pre-industrial era (before 1850) is an objective set by the States at the COP 15 in Copenhagen. According to scientists, 2°C is a threshold that must not be exceeded in order to avoid disastrous consequences for humanity.

talk about economic growth when it leads to the loss of a large forest area? In view of the climate challenge that awaits us, the answer to these questions should be negative; unfortunately, it is still positive today. It is this denial that we denounce.

The aim of this text is to expose this climate hypocrisy so that each of us, with our means, can put pressure on political leaders to change things. Numerous associations, thousands of citizens and even some companies are already engaged in this fight and we hope that this book will bring them additional arguments. Because, as we show in the last chapter, global warming is not inevitable and we have the means to take up this challenge. Another way exists, it is really just a question of choice.

Climate change: between scientific consensus and lack of political action

The scientific consensus on climate change is no longer in doubt. The urgency of climate change is now undeniable. The global warming of the atmosphere - by 0.89°C between 1901 and 2012[3] - is already having adverse effects on people and economic activities around the world, and these effects are likely to worsen significantly in the coming years if we do nothing. As the latest IPCC report[4] indicates, there is more than 95% certainty that climate change is anthropogenic, i.e.,

---

3. Jean JOUZEL and Anne DEBROISE, *Le défi climatique : objectif 2 °C*, Paris, Dunod, 2014.

4. Intergovernmental Panel on Climate Change. The 5th report was published in several volumes during 2013-2014 and its synthesis was released in November 2014.

caused by human activities. It also tells us that the world's atmosphere will warm by an average of at least 4°C compared to the pre-industrial era if we do not act immediately to reduce our greenhouse gas emissions.

Climate change appears to some as a distant problem, both geographically and temporally. Nothing could be further from the truth. The main physical consequences of climate change are already perceptible, such as the increase in the frequency and intensity of extreme weather events[5] (storms, floods, heat waves...), the rise in sea level (already 0.19 meters since 1900) and the melting of the ice cap at a remarkable speed.

Nor should we believe that industrialized countries like ours, are (or will be) spared the consequences of climate change. The year 2014 was the hottest in history, as much in France as for the planet as a whole. France had an exceptional year in terms of natural disasters. The floods in the Hérault region at the end of September 2014, when the equivalent of six months of rain fell in a few hours, are just one example. The current weather conditions clearly show us that climate change is well underway and accelerating. Many economic actors are already worried about it. French farmers, especially wine growers, have taken the measure of the potential consequences on their activity. The Aquitaine region has even commissioned a report on the consequences of climate change on the wine industry by 2050.

---

5. An isolated extreme weather event is not caused by anthropogenic climate change. However, the increased frequency and intensity of such events is a consequence.

Beyond our borders, the consequences of climate change are already having disastrous effects on developing countries. They are at the forefront of the consequences of global warming because of their weaker capacity to adapt but also because of their geographical location. In island states such as Tuvalu, the Maldives or the Philippines, populations are already dealing with the shrinking of their coastal areas as sea levels rise. Natural disasters are particularly devastating in these countries, like what the Philippines suffered with the 2013 supertyphoon Haiyan causing the death of more than 6,000 people. Over the past seven years, an average of 26 million people have had to migrate each year due to natural disasters, more than the number of refugees from wars. In 2014, that number exceeded 40 million people.

These effects of climate change, its human and economic costs will continue to increase if climate runaway is not avoided. In a 2012 report[6] , the World Bank estimated that a world with more than 4°C would lead to a significant increase in poverty, reduced access to water and increased food insecurity. The most affected regions will also be the poorest, such as sub-Saharan Africa and Southeast Asia.

In a December 2014 report, the United Nations Environment Programme estimated that the costs of adapting to climate change in developing countries could fluctuate between $140 billion and $300 billion per year in 2025-2030 and $280 billion to $500 billion

---

6. World Bank, *4 °C: Turn down the heat: Why a 4 °C warmer world must be avoided*, November 2012.

in 2050[7] . These costs could be even higher if we exceed the 2°C target.

To meet the climate challenge, strong measures are needed. To stay below the 2°C limit, scientists recommend a 50% reduction in global CO2 emissions by 2050 compared to 1990 levels, and then reaching zero emissions by 2100 at the latest. Relating CO2 emissions to a budget, humanity would be allowed to emit about 1 trillion tons of CO2 between 1850 and 2100. However, as of 2011, we have already spent 515 billion tons of carbon, or 52% of the budget. Our current emissions trajectory would therefore lead to exceeding this budget before 2035!

Thus, it is still possible to stay below 2°C, but it will require a radical change, as quickly as possible, in our economic model and our lifestyles. The room for maneuver decreases with time. According to scientists, we need to peak our emissions before 2020 and then accelerate our reduction efforts. The problem is that, for the last ten years, they have been growing by an average of 2 to 3% each year and there is no indication in the current production systems and consumption patterns that the reversal of the trend is close. We can therefore only note the difference between, on the one hand, the accumulation of scientific knowledge on the causes and consequences of global warming and, on the other, the weak cooperation between States to fight against it.

---

7. United Nations Environment Programme, *The Adaptation Gap Report*, December 2014.

One only has to look at the content of the various climate conferences to see the extent of the lack of cooperation. First, the Kyoto Protocol, the first and only legally binding agreement, was not ratified by the United States, and then Canada abandoned it midway through without a single sanction being taken.

Secondly, Japan and Europe, once considered good students in the fight against global warming, are far from being exemplary today. Japan has not committed to the second period of the Kyoto Protocol and Europe is lagging behind in the development of clean energy while having an extremely low carbon price.

Thirdly, some industrialized countries, such as Australia and Russia, now have ambiguous (to say the least) positions regarding the fight against climate change. Emerging countries such as China, India and Brazil are claiming their "right to development" and do not wish to commit to binding targets without more effort from those historically responsible for the greenhouse effect. The same is true for developing countries. The latter insist on the responsibility of industrialized countries and demand support to ensure clean development and adaptation to the consequences of climate change.

Finally, at the climate conferences, the way negotiations have traditionally been conducted, based on consensus (and not majority voting), has not allowed for an agreement that is equal to the challenge[8]. In

---

8. The failure of the Copenhagen conference in 2009, where the States were unable to reach an agreement that would follow on from the Kyoto Protocol, is the most flagrant example.

particular, it has given way to a system that favors communications from the various countries on their voluntary objectives and the means to achieve them. But this system is not very conducive to reaching an agreement compatible with the 2°C objective because it has often allowed certain States or groups of States to reduce the ambition and speed of negotiations. For example, at COP 19 in Warsaw, while it was expected that States would submit binding targets for a future agreement at COP 21, several emerging countries managed to get the terminology adopted in the final text to be "a contribution to the agreement" rather than a "commitment[9]". This type of behavior attests to the prominence given to climate issues on the agenda of some countries.

On the issue of support for developing countries, industrialized countries are far from setting a good example. At COP 15 in Copenhagen, they committed to raising 100 billion dollars per year to finance the fight against and adaptation to climate change in the countries of the South. A Green Climate Fund was even created afterwards. However, today, only 10.14 billion dollars have been raised and the Green Fund has still not disbursed anything...

This lack of commitment by industrialized countries is all the more shocking since, by choosing the threshold of 2°C not to be exceeded, the leaders have clearly condemned a part of the island countries. This choice was made at the COP 15 in Copenhagen when

---

9. These contributions are voluntary targets for each country, called *Intended Nationally Determined Contributions* (INDC).

many scientists were saying that if the average temperature of the planet exceeded 1.5°C by 2100, many island countries would disappear. The definition of this type of threshold shows how much climate negotiations are in fact the expression of power relations.

The facts attest to this: there is a huge gap between the increasingly alarming reports of scientists on the one hand, and the action of States to combat global warming on the other. However, logic would suggest that, since it is a matter of preserving a global public good, all countries should cooperate. Unfortunately, the climate issue seems to be of secondary importance and there is clearly a form of denial on the part of the leaders.

Kyoto Protocol: the wrong signal sent by the United States

The Kyoto Protocol is seen as both the greatest achievement and the greatest failure of the international climate negotiations. At COP 3 in 1997 in Japan, states succeeded in agreeing on legally binding targets and deadlines for reducing CO_2 emissions from industrialized countries. This was an undeniable historical achievement. But by refusing to ratify it, the United States sent a very negative signal to the rest of the world about how to deal with the climate problem. Indeed, what can we expect from other countries if the world's leading economic power considers the cost of reducing emissions too high? The loss of credibility in international negotiations and the difficulty since then in reaching a binding agreement with emerging countries are largely due to the defection of the United States.

With the Kyoto agreements, the world went from a convention encouraging countries to stabilize their CO_2[10] emissions to an agreement obliging some of them to reduce them. Obviously, given their historical responsibility, the richest countries, classified in Annex 1[11], were asked to bear the burden. Thus, the protocol aimed at a 5% reduction in greenhouse gas emissions from industrialized countries between 2008 and 2012[12] without imposing any constraints on developing countries (including emerging countries such as China and India).

This distribution of efforts is logical for several reasons: first, industrialized countries are responsible for more than two-thirds of CO_2 emissions in the 20th century; second, the products they consume are mostly manufactured in developing countries; and third, they are the most likely to make the necessary adjustments because they are rich and developed. Several countries had strongly supported the signing of the agreement, notably those of the European Union, Japan, and even the United States at the beginning. This was the first time in history that many of the largest polluters[13] committed to reducing their greenhouse gas emissions.

---

10. United Nations Framework Convention on Climate Change at the Earth Summit in Rio in 1992.

11. Annex 1 is composed of OECD countries (except South Korea and Mexico) and so-called "transition" countries.

12. This was the first period of the Kyoto Protocol. The second, agreed in Doha at COP 18 in 2012, covers the years 2013 to 2020.

13. Canada, United States, Europe, Japan and Russia.

But the United States, which produced 24% of total emissions in 1997 for a population representing only 4.5% of the world's population, decided not to play along. A few weeks after the protocol was signed, the US Senate refused to ratify the treaty by a vote of 95 to zero. The reasons given were the refusal to validate a binding agreement without commitments from developing countries and the risks to the US economy. In the face of this strong opposition, Bill Clinton did not even present the text of the protocol to the Senate and his successor George Walker Bush announced on March 13, 2001, in a letter addressed to four Republican senators, his refusal to regulate greenhouse gas emissions[14].

By judging that the cost to the American economy was too high in comparison to the benefits, and while other rich countries decided to partially subject their economies to the climate constraint, the United States clearly chose to place its economic interests above global well-being. This is not surprising, as George Herbert Walker Bush (Sr.) already stated in 1992 at the Rio conference, in order to oppose a binding agreement, that "the American way of life is not negotiable".

The American position in international negotiations has always been to promote market solutions so as not to challenge the mass consumer society. The development and exchange of green technologies, which would allow the transition of the world economy

---

14. Aurélie VIEILLEFOSSE, *Le changement climatique : quelles solutions*, Paris, "Les Études" n° 5290-5291, La Documentation française, 2009,

to a low-carbon economy, are the main solutions put forward by the United States. The U.S. position is unequivocal: the remedies to climate change are not to be found in a rethinking of American lifestyles and consumption patterns, but in products and their manufacturing processes. Economic growth and mass consumption do not have to change, they only have to become greener.

Of course, it is absolutely essential to invest in and research green technologies, but they should not be a substitute for making efforts to reduce emissions. Especially since the U.S. could achieve a number of energy efficiency gains without overly constraining its lifestyle. By comparison, most rich countries have much lower per capita CO2 emissions than the United States, with almost identical standards of living. For example, in 1997, a British person emitted 9.4 tons of CO2, a Japanese person 9.5 tons, while an American person emitted 19.9 tons. And the real problem is that the American way of life is still the global benchmark, especially in emerging countries.

The behavior of the U.S. government is typically that of the "free rider". By refusing to pay its fair share, the United States - then the largest contributor to global warming - is creating negative externalities for the entire planet. Yet the most violent impacts of climate change will not be for Americans but for the most vulnerable populations of the planet, those for whom the seasons and the climate matter in cultivation, breeding or fishing.

By refusing to implement the Kyoto Protocol, the United States has both delegitimized international climate negotiations and sent the wrong signal to the world's other economies (rich, emerging and developing). As no other country could have done, the United States simply undermined global climate governance. It would probably have been easier to negotiate with emerging countries at subsequent COPs if industrialized countries had been exemplary in implementing the protocol. The resignation of the United States has only complicated the climate negotiations, particularly with China. It also led to an imitation effect on the part of other countries such as Canada, Russia and Japan, which refused a second Kyoto. The United States has also refused to change its position.

Certainly, some American states have made efforts, such as California and several Northeastern states, but the non-application of the Kyoto Protocol has left its mark on the international scene. While the climate issue seemed to be gaining in importance since Rio in 1992, after the defection of the United States, it has once again become a secondary problem, far behind economic issues.

The choice of polluting energies

Despite the awareness of the dangers of global warming, the world has never consumed so much polluting energy. Renewable energies have certainly developed but at almost the same rate as the others and, consequently, still occupy a negligible place in energy balances. Today, more than 80% of the energy used is polluting (oil, gas and coal). These proportions have not changed since 2000.

A look at the evolution of the different energy sources in the last decade is striking. Between 2002 and 2012, oil and gas consumption increased by 14.4% and 31% respectively. Coal consumption, the most polluting energy, increased by 55%! This increase is not entirely attributable to the strong economic and demographic growth of emerging countries. Most developed countries also have their share of responsibility: Canada and Australia now use more oil than ten years ago; the United States, Canada, France and Japan more gas; and the United Kingdom, Poland and Italy consume more coal.

However, this increase in consumption in developed countries cannot be explained solely by economic and demographic growth. Some countries had the capacity to reduce their energy consumption without affecting their standard of living. Studies show that the correlation between HDI (Human Development Index) and annual energy consumption stops at four toe (tons of oil equivalent) per capita. Beyond that, the well-being of individuals no longer increases. However, a number of countries are still above this threshold, such as the United States, Japan, Sweden and Australia. These countries could reduce their energy consumption without affecting their quality of life, so it is no longer a question of necessity but of choice.

Proven reserves of gas and oil have also increased by 21% and 26%, even though the increase in demand should have contributed to the exhaustion of these reserves. The increase in energy prices in the decade 2004-2014 allowed companies to invest massively in research and exploration of the same energies. Governments could have broken this vicious circle by encouraging companies to use this oil rent to finance renewable energy. For example, in the 1970s, after the sharp rise in oil prices, the United States introduced a tax on the unexpected profits of oil companies[15] . From

---

15. Joseph E. STIGLITZ, *Un autre monde. Contre le fatalisme du marché*, Paris, Fayard, 2006, reed. Le Livre de Poche, 2008, p. 247.

2004 onwards, the sustained rise in oil prices allowed companies to generate profits beyond all expectations (even as their production declined). The record profits of 2008 are breathtaking: the top five companies, Exxon, Shell, BP, Chevron and Total, all made profits of more than $20 billion, with Exxon making $45 billion. These companies are all from developed countries - the main culprits of global warming - yet no government of these countries has thought of introducing a tax to finance the energy transition. This unexpected oil windfall could have been a powerful lever to plan for the post-oil era; above all, it has allowed investments in exploration and production to be multiplied by four to find new deposits.

The rise in the price of oil, accompanied by huge investments, has enabled a number of unconventional hydrocarbons to become profitable. This is the case for shale oil and tar sands. Paradoxically, these energies have not been developed in countries that are in a take-off phase, but in rich countries that have long since made the adjustment to a service economy (i.e. one that consumes less energy than industry).

Shale gas is the best example. It has developed massively in the United States thanks in particular to the implementation of the Energy Policy Act, a regulatory framework that is extremely favourable to oil companies, allowing them to be exempted from environmental regulations and to enjoy tax advantages. The results were rapid: in just a few years, the United States added more than 60,000 shale gas wells (i.e. more wells than in the entire Middle East) to reach 500,000 active gas wells in the country. This abundant supply has cut gas prices by a factor of three and has led to improved industrial competitiveness.

This economic success has not gone unnoticed. Canada, a producer of oil from the tar sands, is already in the pre-development phase. As for Europe, considered for a very long time as the good pupil on the issues of global warming and energy transition, a number of countries, such as the United Kingdom or Poland, have not excluded this option...

The issue of Arctic hydrocarbons is also interesting to measure the distance of our governments from the climate issue. While the melting of the ice pack should have alerted states to the dangers of global warming and the need to take emergency measures, it has instead been perceived as an opportunity to go and see if there are hydrocarbons or other raw materials. Companies mainly from developed countries like Shell, Statoil, BP or Total are currently involved in projects.

But the most successful embodiment of climate hypocrisy is found in state subsidies of fossil fuels. In 2014, fossil fuel extraction companies received more than €4.74 trillion in subsidies, the equivalent of ten million euros per minute[16]. This figure is 20 times greater than all investment in renewable energy and greater than all global spending on public health.

Let's not be afraid to say things honestly: if the issue of global warming had not existed, energy production and consumption would have been more or less the

------

16. David P. COADY, Ian PARRY, Louis SEARS, and Baoping SHANG, "How Large are Global Energy Subsidies?", *IMF Working Paper*, no. 15/105, 2015. Read at http://ssrn.com/abstract=2613304.

same. However, with CO2 emissions coming from 80% of fossil fuel combustion, the energy sector should have focused special attention and resources on changing its model. It is clear that despite a consensus on the causes, no action has been taken by governments, especially those of rich countries, to rectify the situation. However, doing nothing in full knowledge of the facts is a choice. Developed countries have clearly chosen to put the climate issue on the back burner.

Blind trust in the market

From the 1990s onwards, politicians have continued to put the market at the center of their decisions. Almost religiously, everyone has come to accept - in accordance with the concept of the invisible hand of the economist Adam Smith - that selfish interests lead to the general interest and that competition is beneficial because it allows for an optimal allocation of resources. Until recently, the European Commission argued in its *Green Paper* "that it was up to the market to find solutions" and that it would support them[17]. The problem is that there is nothing objective about the market, simply because it depends on those who make it up and there may be power struggles between these agents. A review of the last twenty years shows that the logic of the market has not provided any

---

17. European Commission, *Green Paper: building the capital markets union*, February 18, 2015, p. 6.

solutions to combat global warming, nor to initiate the energy transition.

It is interesting to begin by analyzing the consequences of the liberalization of energy markets in Europe. This is a concrete example that shows how blind trust in market mechanisms can lead to results that are radically opposed to those expected. Let us take the case of the United Kingdom, which has often been put forward as an "example to follow" by the European Commission. The liberalization of the British electricity market was intended to break up the public monopolies and allow the appearance of new competitors in order to bring down prices. The results have been radically different. The liberalization process has created an oligopoly of six companies sharing the market in the absence of any credible competitive threat[18] . Obviously, electricity prices, while they were supposed to fall, have risen. In theory, the opening of markets was supposed to benefit the consumer; in practice, it has mainly benefited the companies. The same has been true in France, where electricity prices have risen by an average of 33 per cent since the energy sector was opened to competition in 2007.

We find the same shortcomings when we address the question of price signals. For the defenders of market efficiency, if we want a good or a mode of production to prevail, we must make it less expensive in order to guide consumer choice. It is this argument that has led to the creation of support mechanisms for renewable

---

18. Raphaël Homayoun BOROUMAND, "The Iron Lady, the Invisible Hand and the Electricity Fairy," *Le Monde*, July 15, 2013.

energies (with the aim of making them cheaper) so that they can enter the energy markets, while then allowing competition to operate between the different energies. The problem is that the conditions of competition are extremely unfavorable to renewable energies, even taking into account the support mechanisms.

Renewable energy companies, characterized by a multitude of players in different sectors, face large companies with long-established technologies and infrastructures. It is important to remember that these companies, generally referred to as "incumbents", have developed in a non-competitive environment: a public company with a monopoly[19]. This is the case in France, where the energy system is the product of centralized planning and management, which has given rise to large public companies[20]: EDF, Engie (formerly GDF-Suez), Areva and Total[21]. These companies have sufficient weight to influence market conditions, and renewable energy players - even with the help of support mechanisms - remain at a disadvantage. However, one of the conditions for competition to work is precisely that the players be of identical size (known as atomicity in economics).

---

19. Raphaël Homayoun BOROUMAND, Stéphane GOUTTE and Thomas PORCHER, *20 idées reçues sur l'énergie*, Brussels, "Planète en jeu", De Boeck Supérieur, p. 172.

20. Jean-Marie CHEVALIER, Michel CRUCIANI and Patrice GEOF-FRON, *Energy transition: the real choices*, Paris, Odile Jacob, 2013, p. 33.

21. Even today, EDF, Engie (formerly GDF-Suez) and Areva have a large part of their capital held by the State.

In the case of renewables, long-term policy choices have thus given way to a model that combines support policies and a liberalized market. The results of this model are mixed, to say the least, and the results show that even if renewable energies are developing, they are having difficulty taking market share from traditional energies.

The question is why, if the State sincerely wanted to develop renewables, did it prefer to trust the market rather than play its role as a majority shareholder by pushing incumbent companies into renewable energies? Perhaps because of a belief in the virtues of market efficiency, but probably also because it was facing a well-organized opposition...

The price signal effect is also questioned in the case of non-substitutable goods. This is the case for oil, where the price increase over the decade 2000-2010 had only a marginal effect on consumer behavior. No one would have thought that consumers could bear a price increase from $20 to over $100. But that's what happened. The price increased by a factor of five without naturally triggering a revolution in production and consumption patterns. Price elasticity and cross-price elasticity did not work (or worked very little) because oil is a difficult-to-substitute good. Under these conditions, advocating a price increase to give a price signal in the hope of reducing consumption may not be enough.

Conversely, the price signal has proven to be very effective in the case of the substitution of gas for coal. A certain number of conditions are necessary for competition to operate: the energy sources must be substitutable in their uses and they must be at almost similar levels of development. This is the case for gas and coal. The development of shale gas has led to a drop in the price of gas, making it more advantageous than coal in the United States. The decline in U.S. demand for coal has led to a drop in prices, making it more attractive to Europeans. The result: U.S. coal consumption shifted to Europe. While the price signal worked from a local perspective, from a global perspective it only shifted consumption.

A closed-economy analysis of the U.S. case (i.e., as if it were the only one in the world) would lead to the following result: the price signal was effective because lower gas prices led to a gas-coal substitution effect. But a global analysis (in an open economy) would raise the question of what happened to the good that left the market in a closed economy... On a global scale, there is no difference, just a shift in consumption and associated pollution. Generally speaking, in the absence of development or common regulations, what one country's market loses, another gets back...

Finally, the failure of the carbon market is one of the best examples of the lack of objectivity of markets, or rather of their human construction (therefore non-objective). While the principle of this market was to encourage the most polluting companies to reduce their emissions, it has only been a tool to encourage them not to change because of the extremely low price of carbon. However, the project had started well, it consisted in defining by country carbon emission caps for polluting companies and sectors but then, through the market, it was possible for the most polluting companies to buy the allowances of a company that emits less than its authorized cap. And as emissions allowances were over-allocated (thanks to an effective lobby), the price of carbon fell sharply. The price signal, intended as an incentive to stop polluting, has had the opposite effect[22].

In the end, there is no evidence to date that market mechanisms are effective in dealing with the problem of global warming. Those who advocate integrating negative externalities by transforming them into commodities and creating a market along the lines of the buy-sell system for the right to pollute forget that the amounts of pollution allowed will probably be subject to fierce lobbying that could have the same consequences as the carbon market in Europe. Others who advocate internalizing negative externalities in the price of energy to create price signals know that this method is not consistently effective and is especially complex. Even if there are studies on the financial cost of global warming or diesel, how do we take these externalities into account? Where do they stop? Should the 25 million climate refugees each year be factored into the price of oil, gas and coal? Can we really put a figure on the degradation of nature or health?

It is true that an internalization of the externalities specific to each energy is necessary because it would give a different price to the energies and would allow

---

22. Jean GADREY, "Preserving nature by giving it a price? Les dérives marchandes", to be read on alternatives-économiques.fr/blogs/gadrey/2013/10/23preserving-nature-by-giving-it-a-price-44-the-market-derives/

the carbon-neutral ones to become more competitive. But a more appropriate price signal for energy (and ultimately for goods) should not be the alpha and omega of the fight against global warming. Above all, we need massive investments in renewable energies and in the energy renovation of buildings. However, these investments require States to have a long-term vision that is contrary to the logic of the market.

Free trade treaties against the climate

At each IPCC report or COP meeting, world leaders take turns to call for action in order to provide appropriate responses to avoid climate catastrophe. Each one makes an agreed statement about the energy transition and the need to reduce CO_2 . Yet, at the same time, these leaders are negotiating free trade treaties that disturbingly illustrate the denial of global warming by continuing to separate environment and trade, and worse, by subordinating the former to the latter.

Europe, which has long been considered an exemplary country in the fight against global warming, is not immune to this trend. In 2006, it defined a trade policy strategy aimed at seeking free trade agreements with its main trading partners. This project, called "Global Europe: Competing in the World," has led to the signing of free trade agreements with Peru, Colombia, Honduras, Nicaragua, Panama and Canada. Others are underway with Ukraine, Moldova, Georgia, Armenia or with regional organizations such as the Gulf Cooperation Council or Mercosur[23] . The famous transatlantic partnership with the United States, better known as TAFTA[24] , is also part of this strategy.

The problem is that these treaties, by their principles and consequences, are in direct conflict with the issue of global warming. Above all, they enshrine the trade in goods. What counts is the circulation of goods, regardless of the environmental consequences. Already at the WTO, the perimeter and the term "environment" are awaiting a precise definition and protection. It is true that paragraphs *a* and *b* of Article XX of the GATT allowed states to maintain policies aimed at preserving natural resources and life free of trade barriers. But for various reasons, the word "environment" was never added to subparagraph *b* of the mentioned article. The WTO bases its decisions not on the precautionary principle or any other ethical consideration but on expertise. In other words, everything that concerns the environment or the climate is not taken into account at the WTO. So we end up with leaders who recognize the role of human activity on global warming, advocate the reduction of CO2

---

23. Common market regrouping several South American countries.

24. Thomas PORCHER and Frédéric FARAH, *TAFTA : l'accord du plus fort*, Paris, Max Milo, 2014.

emissions, but voluntarily decide to ignore it when it comes to talking about trade[25].

These treaties, in addition to promoting the multiplication of trade, risk lowering the standards of goods. For one of the particularities of these new generation free trade agreements is that beyond the reduction of customs duties, they extend their scope to all fields of trade and address trade barriers "behind the border", i.e. on standards established within a country.

The aim of these free trade treaties is therefore to achieve an approximation of the standards of the different countries in order to define common standards of production and consumption. The problem is that, under these conditions, if a State decides to impose new regulations aimed at taking environmental costs into account, it will be at a disadvantage compared to those who do not. States, in order to preserve the competitiveness of their industries, may therefore not put in place regulations that take environmental aspects into account, as this would be like running with sandbags.

This government intervention will be all the more limited as competing companies easily agree when their interests converge. If it is a question of lowering standards to make more profit, competing brands are able to act together. We saw in the case of shale gas in France how French or Canadian companies, which were basically competitors, agreed when it came to

----

25. Even though some developed countries are beginning to address some of the climate-related issues at the WTO, notably by accusing emerging countries of environmental dumping.

Free trade treaties against the climate

trying to break the law banning hydraulic fracturing. Under these conditions, it will be difficult to create a model that is environmentally demanding.

Moreover, the treaties provide for mechanisms to fight against the evolution of the rules: arbitral tribunals. This type of tribunal is inspired by the ICSID doctrine[26], which stipulates that a company is entitled to the legal environment it had when it started its business, and therefore has the right to be compensated for the profit lost due to any change in legislation or regulations that would be unfavourable to it. In other words, with the introduction of this mechanism, it will be impossible or very costly for a State to enact new rules by law or regulation. The courts will therefore be a weapon for multinationals, since investors will be able to use them when they feel that the regulatory framework has been modified to their disadvantage.

However, to promote an energy transition and the fight against global warming, it will be necessary to impose restrictions on certain energies (such as the exit from nuclear power in Germany or the ban on hydraulic fracturing in France) while promoting renewable energies, encouraging more sober modes of production via tax incentives and more heavily regulating certain sectors. But all these policies could be seen as barriers to trade or distortions of competition, and the companies concerned could challenge

---

26. The International Centre for Settlement of Investment Disputes (ICSID) is a Washington, D.C.-based body created by the International Bank for Reconstruction and Development (IBRD) that deals with disputes between a state and an investor from another state.

them in arbitration tribunals. In this type of treaty, trade law clearly takes precedence over social or environmental law.

These free trade agreements are therefore further proof of the climate denial of our leaders. These agreements are above all about trade between countries and aim to eliminate all obstacles to the movement of goods. No clause deals with the climate issue and the harmonization of standards risks lowering environmental and social standards. Finally, arbitration tribunals, like a sword of Damocles over the State, offer a legal guarantee to multinationals against regulatory change.

Unsuitable measurement indicators

Measurement indicators play an extremely important role in our societies. They reveal and guide policy choices and influence the behavior of companies and individuals. If these indicators are incomplete, then they inevitably give an erroneous measure of reality and can present dangers for the future. GDP, which measures market production, is today the most widely used measurement tool. However, it has many limitations, such as the fact that it does not take into account the well-being of individuals or the degradation of the environment. A certain number of our accounting measures must evolve, quite simply because they lead economic agents to make bad decisions which, in the end, compromise the future of all.

GDP has been debated since its creation. As Al Gore recalled in a climate conference at Sciences Po in June 2015, "The creator of GDP himself, Simon Kuznets, always insisted that it should not be used as a compass for economic policy, explaining as early as the 1930s that GDP was a limited and inadequate indicator to measure all economic activity." Numerous reports point in this direction, the best known being that of Joseph Stiglitz, Amartya Sen and Jean-Paul Fitoussi on measuring economic performance and social progress[27].

The main finding of the Stiglitz report is that GDP is a very limited measure if we take into account the realities and challenges of the 21st century, namely environmental preservation and poverty reduction. Indeed, the GDP does not take into account pollution, whether atmospheric, noise, industrial or food. It does not take into account the inequalities in the distribution of wealth, which have increased sharply since 1975[28]. Finally, it does not take into account the destruction of natural resources, whether it be deforestation, depletion of raw materials or arable land. Yet these elements are fundamental to ensure the sustainability of an economic activity. If GDP growth leads to the loss of a large area of forest, how is it that this environmental degradation is not taken into account?

Conversely, if GDP growth is due to the adverse consequences of global warming, then why should we consider it an improvement in economic activity? And

---

27. The 2009 "Stiglitz-Sen-Fitoussi Commission" on the measurement of economic performance and social progress.

28. See the work of Thomas PIKETTY on inequality, notably in his latest book: *Le capital au xxie siècle*, Paris, Seuil, 2013.

yet this is the case today when rebuilding roads and homes after tsunamis and other extreme weather events.

The measurement of GDP and its evolution (economic growth) are purely quantitative indicators and therefore by definition limited. What is the point of growth if it is based on the exploitation of polluting energies, on the compression of wages and social rights of employees? The measurement of GDP must be accompanied by other indicators measuring the impacts on the well-being of individuals (the goal of any society) and on the environment (the sustainability of this well-being).

Other indicators send misleading signals that lead us straight into the wall. For example, accounting today allows energy companies to value their hydrocarbon reserves as assets, even though, if we are to have any chance of meeting the 2°C target, the world will not be able to use them all. A study by University College London published in the journal *Nature* showed that to maintain the IPCC targets, one third of proven oil reserves, half of gas reserves and 82% of coal reserves will have to be left in the ground. Under these conditions, how is it possible that accounting can allow these hydrocarbon reserves to be valued financially and thus continue to encourage companies to increase their levels?

The setting of "prices" is another type of measurement that does not reflect reality. Currently, prices depend on production costs, the margin appropriated by the producer and taxes. However, for many products, there are a lot of indirect costs that do not appear in the price or in the companies' balance sheets. For example, the low prices of fruits and vegetables full of pesticides do not include the health costs they generate, the low price of meat from intensive breeding does not include the cost of polluted water or green algae on the Breton coast[29], and the price of coal does not include the costs of pollution...

Yet these indirect costs will be paid by the taxpayer. Health costs due to pollution, the cost of cleaning up beaches or purifying polluted water are all negative externalities that end up being paid for by the taxpayer. So we have a measurement system that, on the one hand, encourages companies to produce goods at low prices without paying the indirect costs of their mode of production and, on the other hand, individuals who are encouraged to buy these products (via competitive prices) and who will pay the indirect costs via taxes. The reduction of regulations is in fact a transfer of part of the cost from companies to households.

Finally, the method of accounting for CO_2 emissions is not fair. It only takes into account the CO_2 emitted on the territory, whereas since the 1990s, we have witnessed a movement of relocation of industries to emerging countries, notably China. By taking into account CO_2 emissions based on consumption (i.e. taking into account exports and imports of goods), we would arrive at fairer measures. How can we ask emerging countries to make efforts on their CO_2 emissions if some of our companies benefit from them and if we consume the goods manufactured in these conditions?

---

29. Marc DUFUMIER, *50 idées reçues sur l'agriculture et l'alimentation*, Paris, Allary Éditions, 2014.

An approach based on accounting for emissions consumed would be less hypocritical and would provide a greater incentive to change our behavior. This would not exempt emerging countries from making efforts to fight global warming (in particular by stopping subsidizing fuel prices), but it would provide a better vision of everyone's responsibilities. Remember that one of the principles of the climate convention is "common but differentiated responsibility". In order to reach an agreement that is acceptable to all, it must be considered fair and equitable. A good start would be to complement the measurement of greenhouse gas emissions with the measurement of emissions consumed.

The choice of measurement indicators is really more political than technical. If we blindly rely on the GDP growth rate, then we expose ourselves to future economic, social and ecological crises. Let's not forget that before the subprime crisis, the United States had a high growth rate that was not sustainable in the long term. The subprime crisis has left enormous after-effects from which we in Europe have still not recovered. The short-term vision of profit and growth alone can lead us straight into the wall. It is imperative to add other measures that take into account the well-being, the environment and the sustainability of our economic activities.

But we must not be naïve: better measurement indicators are a necessary but not sufficient condition to ensure an effective fight against climate disruption. As we have seen in the first chapter, there are many measurements and studies that indicate the urgency of taking action. The work of Nicholas Stern, a British economist and former vice president of the World Bank, has shown that as a percentage of GDP, the cost of inaction would be much higher than that of action. According to the economist, the cost of fighting climate change would be estimated at only 1% of GDP per year compared to 5 to 20% of global GDP if we exceed 2°C of warming. The 2006 Stern Review is extremely useful because, for the first time, it provided an economic assessment of the consequences of climate change using GDP, the most familiar indicator. Nothing better to convince leaders to act. The lack of action by our leaders despite the international resonance of this report teaches us that while better metrics are needed to know where we are going, they are useless if no one is paying attention.

UNITED STATES/CHINA: THE INSIGNIFICANT AGREEMENT

The refusal of the United States to ratify the Kyoto Protocol and China's refusal to make binding commitments on its CO2 emissions have severely stalled progress in international climate negotiations. In November 2014, these two countries (often referred to as the climate G2) announced a climate change agreement committing to a decline in U.S. emissions by 2025 and a peak in China's emissions by 2030. This was a first for China and the first climate agreement in history between the two countries. It thus seems to be a "historic" step forward, if only because it attests to the fact that the world's two largest emitters of greenhouse gases (41% of global emissions between them) are taking the problem into account. Unfortunately, beyond the symbolism and with regard to the 2°C objective, the measures taken by the two countries remain largely insufficient and this agreement does not necessarily send a good signal to other countries on how to deal with the climate issue.

Despite being the world's largest and second largest economies respectively, the United States and China are countries with radically different levels of development and economic structure. China emits 9.9 billion tons of CO_2 compared to 5.2 billion tons for the U.S., but its population is 1.3 billion compared to 316 million for the U.S., which means that an American emits three times more CO_2 than a Chinese[30] .

CO_2 emissions per unit of GDP are also much higher in China than in the United States. This is mainly due to the fact that the US has a distribution of economic sectors that is largely in favor of the tertiary sector (services): it accounts for 79.6 percent compared to 34.1 percent for China. Energy intensity, which measures global energy consumption per unit volume of GDP, is higher in the primary and secondary sectors than in the tertiary sector. The structure of Chinese economic activity is by definition more CO_2 emissions intensive, and its shift to a service economy, as is the case in developed economies today, should reduce its energy intensity.

The United States and China, although close in rankings, are in reality two completely different economies, and the average Chinese person does not live nearly as well as an American. This gap was even wider in 1997 when the Kyoto Protocol was ratified. Under

---

30. 17.5 tons of CO_2 per capita for an American versus 6.19 for a Chinese.

these conditions, one can imagine the complexity of the debates at climate conferences. When the United States asked China to make a commitment to combat global warming, China returned the argument of per capita emissions and the fact that the United States, like all industrialized countries, has a historical carbon debt. Let's remember that in the 20th century, OECD countries were responsible for two thirds of global emissions. Under these conditions, it is easy to understand why it has been so difficult to reach an agreement over the past 15 years and why most observers have described the agreement between the United States and China as "historic."

But in substance, the objectives of the agreement announced by Barack Obama and Xi Jinping are rather banal, if not almost insignificant. For the first time, China commits to a peak in greenhouse gas emissions around 2030 with the intention of "trying to get there sooner". It also announced a target of 20% clean energy in its energy production by 2030. The U.S. has committed to reducing its greenhouse gas emissions by 26 to 28 percent from 2005 levels by 2025.

However, these objectives are still largely insufficient to stay below the 2°C of warming advocated by the IPCC. Apart from the fact that for the first time the United States and China have managed to reach an agreement, the agreement is not historic. As far as China is concerned, a peak "around 2030" is a distant date that does not prevent it from continuing to increase its emissions for about fifteen years. In fifteen years, China's economy will gradually shift from secondary to tertiary. CO_2 emissions will decrease with the deformation of economic activity. In reality, what China is proposing is not to set any constraints on its development, as the industrialized countries did in the 20th century. Setting a peak at 2030 is tantamount to giving itself the right to develop without taking global warming into account, even though all the experts recommend that the peak of Chinese emissions must occur well before 2030 in order to meet the IPCC's objectives. The IPCC also recommends 2020 as the necessary date for the global peak in emissions.

For the United States, the goal of a 26-28% reduction in greenhouse gas emissions by 2025 compared to 2005 would correspond to a reduction of only 10-15% compared to 1990 (the base year used by Europe and most other developed countries). In comparison, Europe has set a target of reducing its emissions by at least 40% in 2030 compared to 1990. For its part, the IPCC recommends a reduction in emissions from industrialized countries of 80 to 95% by 2050 compared to 1990. The United States is far from these objectives today.

It is clear that the success of COP 21 does not depend solely on the commitment of the G2 and Europe. The commitment of all developed and emerging countries is crucial. However, since COP 15 in Copenhagen, we have noticed that some developed countries are increasingly reluctant. This is the case of Canada, which withdrew from the Kyoto Protocol when it was unable to reach its first objective. But also Japan, which has not committed to a second Kyoto. Australia, since the election of Prime Minister Tony Abbott in September 2013, has been moving backwards on climate and environmental issues in a worrying way. The opposition between ecological transition and economic growth is Mr. Abbott's main argument, which demonstrates archaic thinking. Climate sceptic statements, cancellation of the national carbon tax, weakening of the budget for environmental policy... there is no shortage of examples to demonstrate his and the government's hostility towards climate and environmental preservation. Australia could be a formidable opponent in the battle for Paris.

The same is true for Russia. In addition to its hostile position to the second Kyoto period, its contribution to the COP 21 agreement submitted in April 2015 attests to a commitment that is ambiguous, to say the least. Certainly, it does show a target of 25% to 30% reduction in greenhouse gas emissions compared to 1990 by 2030, but by including the absorption of CO2 by its forests in the calculation methodology. In this way, Russia can exempt itself from some of the efforts needed to reduce the carbon intensity of its economy.

Emerging countries such as Brazil, India, Mexico and South Africa will also play a key role in the Paris climate negotiations. Yet their engagement has been mixed so far. From an energy transition perspective at the national or local level, we see some positive trends, such as the significant development of renewable energy in South Africa, Brazil and India. For example, India set a target of 100 GW of solar electricity production by 2022 in 2015 and will finance this development by increasing taxes on fossil fuels. However, the commitments of emerging countries are not yet concrete enough in the arena of international negotiations. Holding the

United States/China: the insignificant agreement

argument that they are the historical leaders of climate change who must first set an example, they have never made binding, quantified commitments to reduce their greenhouse gas emissions.

Nor should the OPEC countries of the Middle East be excluded from their responsibility in the fight against climate change. It is undeniable that their economic model is based on the exploitation of their oil and gas resources and that a quantified commitment on greenhouse gas emissions is not in their interest. However, it should be noted that some of these countries, notably Qatar and the United Arab Emirates, seem to have been willing to engage in research on renewable energy and energy efficiency for several years. The creation of Masdar in Abu Dhabi, a 100% renewable energy transition laboratory city, is one of several projects that reveal a certain sensitivity on the part of these countries to the energy transition, even if at the international level, like the others, no quantified commitment has been made.

Thus, the landscape of international climate cooperation is much more complex today than it was six years ago. Unlike in Copenhagen, the focus is no longer solely on China, the United States and Europe, but on all actors. We are facing a more horizontal dynamic with fewer and fewer undisputed leaders.

The success of COP 21 will therefore depend on the commitment of all countries - developed, emerging and even developing. Taking into account the diversity of development levels and socio-economic conditions, it would be relevant to review the categorization of countries in the convention because it is no longer logical that a country like Chad, with almost zero CO2 emissions per capita, is in the same category (outside of Annex 1) as the United Arab Emirates, which has some of the highest emissions per capita on the planet.

Nevertheless, particular attention remains on the United States and China. By announcing targets, they can encourage other reluctant countries to do so. On the other hand, by maintaining a bilateral relationship and setting soft targets on arbitrarily set reference years, they delegitimize climate conferences and show the international community that the climate issue can be managed as the French expression goes: "Où tu veux, quand tu veux, comme tu veux.

LET'S GET OUT OF DENIAL AND TAKE UP THE CLIMATE CHALLENGE

Until now, the States have preferred the posture of climate denial rather than that of challenge. Successive COPs have failed to sign a universal (committing all countries), binding (obliging countries to respect their commitments) and ambitious (enough to reach the 2°C objective) climate agreement. The objective of the COP 21 is to remedy this.

However, it is highly likely that COP 21 will produce an agreement that is binding in form rather than in substance. Instead of committing to binding numerical targets for reducing greenhouse gas emissions, countries will probably commit to taking action at the national level and reporting on it regularly. The Obama administration seems to favor this type of agreement because it would not require Senate ratification[31] and could be implemented at the national level through executive action.

Thus, the binding aspect of the agreement will probably be limited to the minimum commitment by states and will leave room for subsequent communications on their voluntary national targets[32] . This type of commitment will allow the international community and the general public to better follow and compare the contributions of each country. The goal is to generate pressure on countries that have insufficient targets, according to the principle of the *name and shame game.*

But this game of pressure on bad performers will only work if some countries take radical measures. It is in this context that we are making ten breakthrough proposals. Some can be implemented individually by each state, others will require a global commitment to be part of an agreement. The purpose of this chapter is simply to show that we have the means to confront global warming, that another pathway exists and that it is up to the world's leaders to commit to it as soon as possible.

---

31. Remember that two-thirds of the votes in the Senate are needed to ratify an international treaty in the United States.

32. At COP 20 in Lima, the States committed themselves to making voluntary commitments and to communicating them during 2015. These communications corresponded to "contributions" to the COP 21 agreement and made it possible to evaluate, before its opening, the global effort in the fight against climate change.

1. Understand that the fight against global warming is not the enemy of economic activity

The fight against climate change is an economic opportunity, not a constraint. Job and wealth creation in the green economy is proven in many countries. The costs of clean technologies and energy are constantly decreasing. Protecting the environment reduces health costs for citizens and communities. And businesses are more competitive when they are more resource efficient.

But to do this, it is essential to change the indicators of measurement. As we saw earlier, growth is far from being a perfect indicator; other measures must be added to complement it. The main problem with this indicator is that it does not distinguish good growth from bad growth. An increase in coal production should be counted differently in economic growth because it is a regression in the evolution of energy systems. Similarly, should an increase in cereal production be counted in the same way, knowing that current production allows us to feed 11 billion people, while the world population is seven billion and two billion people suffer from hunger? In this case, it is clear that the problem is one of distribution rather than growth and that producers should be encouraged to increase quality rather than volume.

On the other hand, growth in renewable energy, green technologies and energy efficiency sectors is needed. It is essential to supplement the measurement of growth with other indicators that can better differentiate between good and bad growth. We could even go further, as the German energy company E.ON has done, by accounting differently for old world activities (high carbon cost activities) and new world activities (low carbon cost activities). Furthermore, it is essential to promote the creation of jobs in these green sectors and, above all, to support - with appropriate training - the conversion of existing jobs, particularly in sectors destined to decline such as fossil fuels.

2. Act to get agreement rather than wait for agreement to act

The blockages at the various climate conferences come mainly from the fact that most countries refuse to make efforts if the others do not. Each country assumes that its individual efforts will be useless if they represent a small share of total greenhouse gas emissions. This vision is in fact extremely simplistic because it neglects the interdependence and imitation effects between countries. If Europe fully embraces the energy transition and refuses to consume imported products with high carbon costs, it will force other countries to adapt and eventually lead them towards more sober production mechanisms. This phenomenon would be even stronger if it came from the world's leading power, the United States. Moreover, the industrialized countries would be in a better position to negotiate with the emerging countries if they were themselves exemplary in the fight against global warming.

Rather than a proactive stance, the prevailing position today is that of the "free rider", which consists of doing as little as possible while benefiting from the efforts of others. This posture has proven to be counterproductive, as shown by the little progress made since the Kyoto Protocol at the various COPs. However, throughout the world, many non-state actors have already committed themselves: this is the case of several local authorities. In July 2015 in Lyon, UCLG (United Cities and Local Governments) organized a World Summit of Local Authorities on Climate to show that territories are ready to accelerate the ecological transition. Leaders must encourage and drive this commitment from local governments by promoting their capacity to experiment and carry out projects.

3. Massive development of renewable energies

As we have seen, polluting energies have developed enormously over the last fifteen years. Renewable energies have also progressed, but not enough to take market share from traditional energies. We have to admit that our energy balance has not changed much since the end of the 20th century.

One of the first things to do would be to redirect fossil fuel subsidies to renewable energies. Then, the State should commit itself more voluntarily to their deve-lopment. Let's remember that energy development is extremely political. Market forces would never have allowed the nuclear industry to develop as much as it has in France. The share of nuclear power in our energy balance sheet depends mainly on the support of the State, which has been fully committed to this energy since the 1960s. Today, governments should choose the new winners (renewable energies and energy efficiency) as they did before with other energies.

The first argument used to slow down this transition is the cost of renewable energies compared to traditional energies. But this argument no longer holds. The Deutsche Bank estimates that solar energy is as competitive as coal, gas or nuclear energy on half of the world market, and the production cost of photovoltaic energy has been divided by eight in twenty years[33] . The decreasing costs of renewable energies while they are still in the learning phase are all signals that indicate that they are a sector of the future. Renewable energies will be all the more competitive if their development is associated with the renovation of buildings, which will lead to a reduction in the volume of energy consumed and, ultimately, in household bills.

The second argument is the intermittence of renewable energies such as solar and wind power (solar only produces energy during the day and wind turbines only when there is wind). But this reason is only a scarecrow because it is possible to put forward renewable energies and then use gas power plants as a *backup to* smooth out the production of energy at first while waiting for electricity storage technologies, which are being industrialized[34] , to be developed on a large scale[35] .

---

33. Pascal CANFIN and Peter STAIME, *30 questions pour comprendre la conférence de Paris*, Paris, Éditions Les petits matins, 2015.

34. Just look at Tesla's latest battery.

35. This does not mean to promote the development of gas but to insert temporarily in a pro-renewable energy system the gas in the role of support to the intermittency.

Finally, it is important to note that the renewable energy sector is as competitive as it is job-creating, especially compared to non-renewable energy. A study by the University of Massachusetts shows that an investment of one million euros creates 19 jobs in energy efficiency, 14 in renewable energies and 5 in nuclear energy[36] . The solutions are therefore within reach and the energy revolution is underway, it is now up to leaders to ensure that the speed of the transition accelerates.

4. Invest in the efficiency and control of our energy consumption

The cleanest energy is that which is not consumed. Energy sobriety, which is based on efficiency and control of our energy consumption, is the second pillar of the energy transition and must benefit from an ambitious policy. Improving energy efficiency can be done in several sectors, such as energy production, industry, agriculture, transport or buildings, and can increase the competitiveness of companies and the purchasing power of citizens.

In the building sector, significant gains are possible through energy renovation. In France, buildings are responsible for 44% of energy consumption and 25% of greenhouse gas emissions. The President of the Republic had set a renovation target of 500,000 homes per year. We are still far from achieving this goal. The

---

36. Political Research Institute, University of Massachusetts.

main argument is that renovations are expensive and that the State does not have enough money to undertake a large public financing program for buildings. This argument is false for two reasons.

The first is that reducing the energy consumption of buildings generates gains for the state. The example of Germany is convincing. An IDDRI study shows that for every euro invested in renovation, the German government recovers two to four euros through taxes due to the activity generated. There is nothing economically unhealthy about public spending when you invest in sectors that provide a return on investment.

The second reason is that some countries, such as France, have access to financing with extremely low interest rates, which is very conducive to economic recovery in these sectors of the future. As for emerging or poor countries, which have less easy access to financing, it is essential that rich countries support them by raising public and private funds, in particular via the Green Fund. We must also ensure that financing is easier to obtain for low-carbon projects and that construction companies in industrialized countries commit to minimum energy efficiency standards, including in their projects with Southern countries.

Finally, the energy renovation of buildings must be as passive (by insulating roofs, windows, etc.) as it must be active (allowing real control of consumption by manufacturers or households). In this respect, a large investment and the availability of energy management technologies are necessary. These innovations must also be rapidly disseminated to emerging or poor countries by easing the intellectual protection regime. All the technologies that allow consumers to control their demand are real revolutions and will make it possible to make significant energy savings. Even if technical progress is not the only solution and many people put it forward to avoid the other efforts needed, it is clear that its role in the fight against global warming is undeniable.

5. Putting a fair and equitable price on carbon

As we explained earlier, the price signal is not always effective and setting a carbon price will not be the miracle solution to fight global warming. Nevertheless, it remains a relatively effective instrument as long as certain rules are respected. The example of the European carbon market has shown us that the creation of a global market could prove to be a difficult exercise, particularly because the setting of CO_2 quotas would lead to numerous debates and it is easy to imagine that, under pressure from the various States, these quotas would be over-allocated, leading to the same effects as the European carbon market, i.e. a derisory price.

A tax would be much more effective, but if each state has to set it, then it is possible that some states will have an incentive to cancel the tax through subsidies and thus play the tax competition game. Finally, a uniform carbon tax set by a multilateral body would probably not be supported by all because it would be considered unfair given the inequalities in development between countries.

A progressive carbon price according to the level of development could be a fairer and therefore more easily acceptable solution. The idea is to set a reference carbon price according to the HDI (Human Development Index) and the CO2 emissions consumed[37] . For a given HDI level, countries would therefore pay a carbon price according to a reference price set by a multilateral organization. If the country consumes more emissions than the level attributed to its HDI level then it will pay a higher carbon price than the reference price set in the scale. As the reference carbon price increases with the HDI, emerging countries will have more incentive to rapidly develop green energy and invest in low-carbon systems. Finally, rich countries will pay a higher carbon price and thus have an incentive to accelerate their energy transition.

Setting such a carbon price would make it possible to respect the principle of "common but differentiated responsibility" of the climate convention, but also to avoid opposing competitiveness and the fight against global warming, since the most sober production systems will be those that pay the lowest carbon price.

6. Protect biodiversity and ecosystems

It is impossible to fight effectively against climate change without at the same time fighting against the loss of biodiversity. Preserving biodiversity means limiting global warming and vice versa. Biodiversity

---

37. See the article by Raphaël Homayoun BOROUMAND, Thomas PORCHER and Thomas STOCKER, "COP 21: pour un prix du carbone équitable et progressif," *Le Monde*, September 9, 2015.

and ecosystems are natural carbon sinks, like forests, algae or plankton. They ensure a balance and a good functioning of the natural cycles of the planet, allowing it to better adapt to climate changes.

However, the biodiversity crisis is glaring and getting worse. As the WWF report released in September 2014 demonstrates, half of the world's animal species have disappeared in the last 40 years. According to *the Millennium Ecosystem Assessment,* 60% of the world's ecosystems are degraded due to human activity[38] .

The international community is mobilized on this issue. As with climate change, international negotiations on biodiversity are held every year within the framework of the United Nations Convention on Biological Diversity (CBD, signed at the Rio Earth Summit in 1992, at the same time as the climate convention). France is in the process of transposing certain provisions of the CBD into national law in its bill on the protection of biodiversity, currently being examined by Parliament.

Beyond their role in global warming, biodiversity and ecosystems provide services to humans, called eco-systemic services, which are either irreplaceable or very expensive to reproduce. These services are either irreplaceable or very expensive to reproduce. For example, biodiversity can be used to clean up the pollution of a business zone or nearby waterways. In 1997, several researchers, including Robert Costanza, estimated the value of these ecosystem services at $33,000 billion per year worldwide (compared to a global GDP of

---

38. *Millennium Ecosystem Assessment,* 2005.

$18,000 billion)[39] . Ecological engineering-an approach to engineering that involves harnessing scientific ecology-and bio-mimicry-improving products and production methods through observation of animals and plants-are also tremendous opportunities for technological innovation and job creation. The airplane, whose construction was inspired by bird watching, is an example of this.

The fight against global warming and the preservation of biodiversity are therefore two sides of the same coin. It is essential to adopt a global approach.

7. Activate the lever of education and higher education

Climate change and biodiversity loss are complex phenomena. Giving a head start to future generations is essential. Especially since, if we fail to solve the environmental problems, it is the young people of today who will bear the brunt of the consequences.

Education for the environment and sustainable development is not new. States addressed the subject at the Rio Earth Summit in 1992 by adopting several articles that deal with the importance of education and science on the environment, as well as access to education, especially for women and children in poor countries. In France, the first circular on environmental education dates from 1977. Today, it is important to carry out an

---

39. Robert COSTANZA *et al*, "The value of the world's ecosystem services and natural capital," *Nature*, vol. 387, 15 May 1997, pp. 253-260.

"ecological revision" of all school programs. It is essential to educate children about the challenges of climate and biodiversity with a multidisciplinary approach. Encouraging more school outings and contact with nature, from kindergarten to high school, is a solution that should not be overlooked. Numerous studies on schooling show that this brings benefits for the student, in addition to a sensitivity to environmental protection.

Progress has been made in higher education in taking the environment into account. The proliferation of scientific reports and the inclusion of environmental economics and law in many university and business school curricula attest to this. However, ecology still often remains a disciplinary niche or a cause carried by too few teachers. It is far from being treated in a transversal manner. Disciplines such as micro and macroeconomics, business and finance must now integrate ecological issues. The same is true for business and public finance education, which still compartmentalize climate and environmental issues too much. Mandatory training and testing for teachers and students in universities and business schools could be considered.

8. Defining a new economic model: the circular economy

For more than two centuries, we have developed a linear economy. It is based largely on the extraction of resources, the transformation of these materials to produce products, the consumption of these goods and finally the production of waste. We are making progress in the area of recycling, but our model remains largely linear. Waste contributes to 3% of greenhouse gas emissions each year, but this does not take into account the emissions generated by resource extraction. To give a national example, each inhabitant in France produces 354 kilos of household waste per year[40] . On a global scale, we even observe a sixth continent of waste in the oceans.

However, the ecological footprint is not only downstream but also upstream of our consumption. Natural resources are drastically decreasing all over the planet. The Earth provides mankind and other living beings with a quantity of natural resources that are renewable unless we overconsume. This is a sort of "ecological budget". However, since the 1970s, man has exceeded this budget every year, and earlier and earlier: in 2000, this day was November 1; in 2005, October 20; in 2014, August 19; and in 2015, August 13. It is undeniable that our consumption is increasingly straining the planet's capacity. If the seven billion people who populate it lived like an American, it would take five planets, three if they lived like a French person. Only a change in economic model and in our relationship to consumption can rectify this.

This is why the circular economy must be the economic model of the 21st century. Initially, this will rely on the eco-design of products. This means designing and manufacturing a product in such a way as to anticipate its end-of-life and the reuse of its

____

40. Zero Waste France.

components. Ecodesign opens up a vast field of possibilities in terms of innovation. Of course, programmed obsolescence, i.e. the opposite of eco-design, should simply be prohibited, as France has just enacted in its law on energy transition for green growth (adopted in Parliament at the end of July 2015).

Secondly, the circular economy requires recycling, reusing and recovering materials as much as possible. Waste should no longer be perceived as such but as a resource. This circular approach can be applied in all economic sectors, whether it is for industrial products (e.g., putting construction materials back into production), food products (e.g., making compost and thus returning bio-waste to the earth) or energy resources (e.g., storing and sharing locally produced renewable energy). Not only does this model lead to less resource extraction and manufacturing, and thus less greenhouse gas emissions and environmental degradation, but it also strengthens the competitiveness of economic actors. Industry and agriculture that are efficient in the use of energy, water and raw materials are much more efficient and more protected from the volatility of resource prices. According to the MacArthur Foundation, the circular economy could generate savings of $630 billion for Europe by 2025[41].

Finally, the circular economy is particularly compatible with several other economic models that are environmentally and socially virtuous. The circular economy is more economically interesting when it uses short circuits of manufacturing, reuse

---

41. MacArthur Foundation, *Towards a Circular Economy*, 2012.

and transportation of resources. It lends itself to an economy of proximity, which thus reduces the ecological footprint and promotes social ties. Because it favors local activities, at lower costs and involving resource sharing, the circular economy is often implemented by associations or companies of the social and solidarity economy (SSE). It is not surprising that the SSE shows more stability in the face of economic conditions than the traditional economy. Even with the 2008 crisis, jobs in the social and solidarity economy have grown by 23% over the last ten years in France. Finally, the circular economy encourages the rental of goods, rather than their purchase.

Social economy, collaborative economy, sharing economy, functionality economy... these are the terms used for these parallel economies which are becoming more and more widespread and which deserve to be generalized. All of them allow to boost local activity, to put people back at the heart of the activity and to directly or indirectly reduce their ecological footprint. They open the way to a more resource-efficient consumption and to more sustainable economic activities. In the same way that our planet is characterized by natural cycles, human activity must close the loops and relocalize.

9. Subjecting the WTO and free trade treaties to IPCC objectives

Currently, free trade treaties and the WTO do not include any clause on climate and only address this issue through trade in environmental goods and services. We need to go much further by subjecting this trade to the 2°C climate constraint and by establishing a real normative code on the processes and production methods of traded goods with a dual environmental and social concern. The aim is to reorient the principles and objectives of free trade so that they are open to the three pillars of sustainable development as conceived in 1987 in the Brundtland report (entitled *Our Common Future*): the economic, social and ecological pillars. In this way, the separation that the WTO maintains between trade and environment would disappear.

Under this condition, trade flows would make it possible to converge towards a more demanding model in terms of the environment and social rights. And to avoid using it as a lever for protectionism to prevent developing countries from participating in trade, cleaner technology transfers accompanied by financial compensation (notably through the Green Fund) could be proposed to these countries.

Under these conditions, the space for competition would be voluntarily reduced. It would be done under the constraint of climate and higher standards. From the point of view of economics, this is not exceptional, and the economic history of the last two centuries shows us that we have imposed many limits on the market by prohibiting child labor, reducing working hours, etc. But today, these limits are widely accepted in many countries and tend to spread. Today, however, these limits are widely accepted in many countries and are tending to spread to countries in the process of industrialization. Currently, in most countries, no one would dream of making a 6 year old child work, and countries that have regulations that are too permissive with child labor are regularly denounced. In order for competition to be effective in the short and long term, it must be carried out in a controlled manner. Subjecting the WTO to the IPCC objectives would be a major step forward.

10. Create a G7 for the environment

As we said earlier, the world of tomorrow must no longer be developed according to the same criteria. Economic activity and cooperation at all levels - global, national and local - must integrate climate, environmental and social data much more effectively. This must be done in the existing forums - the COPs, the WTO meetings, the G7, the G20, the Davos Forum. But the urgency forces us to think of new tools that could accelerate the ecological transformation of the world economy.

The G7 is considered the grouping of the world's largest economic powers. Among other criteria (geopolitical, military...), GDP is a determining factor in the selection of countries that belong to it. In the light of the environmental and social challenges of the 21st century, this choice shows a certain archaism in the interpretation of economic performance and the well-being of citizens. Without advocating its disappearance, it is nevertheless useful to create a G7 for the environment that will serve as a complement, or even a counter-power to the traditional G7. This grouping should be based on criteria that take into account the climate, the environment, public health, the redistribution of wealth and the general well-being of the inhabitants. Numerous studies exist to evaluate the candidate countries for such a group. The *World Happiness Report* coordinated by Jeffrey Sachs in 2015 mentions several countries that have implemented policies based on the well-being of their inhabitants and the preservation of the environment, such as Bhutan. The *Happy Planet Index* study by the New Economics Foundation ranked countries according to life expectancy, well-being and ecological footprint. Costa Rica comes first (the United States in 105th position, France and Germany in 50th and 46th positions). This group would take into account valuable environmental resources for the planet, such as the Amazon forest.

The objective of this environmental G7 would be to advance the new economic, social and environmental paradigm, by disseminating good practices, making common commitments, and shifting intellectual software more quickly.

Conclusion

For twenty years, scientific knowledge on climate change has been accumulating. Today, no one can ignore the causes and consequences of our activity on the planet. However, leaders are locked into climate denial by continuing to develop (and subsidize) polluting energies, by ratifying treaties that promote international trade without a climate clause, and by relying on the market to provide miraculous technologies.

It is clear that it is simpler to propose solutions at the margins on the pretext that without a universal agreement, there is no point in fully engaging in the fight. These are the positions held by all leaders today, even though they are harming tens of millions of people on the planet and leading us straight to collective suicide.

However, as we have shown in this book, the solutions exist and we do not have to wait for a climate agreement to be reached at a COP before applying them. Climate change is not inevitable and we have the means to meet the 2°C target by 2100. It is, in fact, only a question of choice. If we choose to lock ourselves into conformity, then the battle is lost. As we have seen, conformity leads at best to climate hypocrisy and at worst to simple denial. Taking up the climate challenge requires courage and first of all the courage to conceive that another economic and social paradigm is possible. We cannot repeat it often enough: we have the means to initiate this change, we just need the political will.

The fight against global warming does not stop at the COP and is an everyday struggle that must be waged in many negotiating forums and by all actors and citizens. Millions of them - from rich and poor countries alike - are engaged in this fight around the world. The COP 21 in Paris will be a moment where the spotlight will be on climate issues, let's mobilize and show our leaders, before it is definitely too late, that we want another future for our children.

KEYWORDS

Carbon or carbon equivalent: Greenhouse gases have different atmospheric lifetimes and different warming powers. In order to measure the global impact of all greenhouse gases, scientists convert them all into carbon dioxide (CO_2 equivalent). We thus speak of carbon emissions or carbon equivalent to refer to all greenhouse gas emissions.

Climate change: Natural phenomena that result from many physical factors on Earth, including the greenhouse effect. These natural phenomena are also called climate disruption or warming. The climate and its evolution are measured over time and not on a daily basis. Thus the climate does not correspond to the weather.

COP: The *Conference of the Parties (COP) is the* two-week annual United Nations climate change negotiations. The COP brings together the 195 states and one regional body (196 parties) that are signatories to the United Nations Framework Convention on Climate Change (UNFCCC). At the end of 2015, the [21st] COP will be held under the presidency of France.

UNFCCC: The United Nations Framework Convention on Climate Change is the international convention developed in 1992 at the Earth Summit and today signed by 196 parties. It is the framework for international climate negotiations and sets as its main objective for the international community to stabilize greenhouse gas emissions in order to prevent climate change from spiraling out of control.

Greenhouse effect: A natural phenomenon that results from the interaction between the atmosphere and the heat flows coming from the Earth. The greenhouse effect allows the atmosphere to retain heat coming from the Sun and sent back by the Earth. Without the greenhouse effect, the global surface temperature would be -18°C on average. However, human activity also contributes to the greenhouse effect because of greenhouse gas emissions. These have increased significantly since the industrial revolution.

Greenhouse gases: Gases that contribute to the greenhouse effect. The main greenhouse gases are water vapor, carbon dioxide, methane, nitrous oxide, ozone and halogenated hydrocarbons. The first five occur naturally in the atmosphere. However, carbon dioxide, methane and nitrous oxide, as well as halogenated hydrocarbons are strongly emitted by human industrial or agricultural activities.

IPCC: The Intergovernmental Panel on Climate Change. Founded in 1987 by the United Nations Environment Program and the World Meteorological Organization, the group brings together more than 2,000 scientists from around the world, including 800 lead authors, to collaboratively research and publish reports on climate change, its causes and consequences. The IPCC finalized its 5th report in late 2014, finding that the climate change we are experiencing is strongly caused by human activities, with 95% certainty.

Acknowledgements

Henri Landes:

I dedicate this book to the CliMates and the members of the French Network of Students for Sustainable Development and particularly thank Florent Baarsch, Astrid Barthélemy, Nicolas Benvegnu, Antonin Briard, Louisa Casson, Marianne Greenwood, Margot Le Guen, Johann Margulies , Marguerite Culot, Mélina Longpré and Thomas Spencer.

Thomas Porcher:

My thanks go to Sarah Salesse, Simon Porcher, Raphaël Boroumand, Stéphane Goutte and Frédéric Farah for their demanding proofreading and their precious advice.

Table of Contents

Best sellers Max Milo Editions

Hitler's banker, Jean-François Bouchard

Confessions of a forger, Éric Piedoie Le Tiec

The Koran and the flesh, Ludovic-Mohamed Zahed

Governing by fake news, Jacques Baud

Governing by chaos, Collectif

A political history of food, Paul Ariès

Mad in U.S.A.: The ravages of the "American model",
Michel Desmurget

Mondial soccer club geopolitics, Kévin Veyssière

Putin: Game master?, Jacques Braud

Treatise on the three impostors: Moses, Jesus, Muhammad,
The Spirit of Spinoza

TV Lobotomy, Michel Desmurget